Sanjeev Kapoor's

# Salads

In association with Alyona Kapoor

www.popularprakashan.com

Published by
POPULAR PRAKASHAN PVT. LTD.
301, Mahalaxmi Chambers
22, Bhulabhai Desai Road
Mumbai - 400 026
for Khana Khazana Publications Pvt. Ltd.

(4077)
ISBN: 978-81-7991-329-1

Photography: Bharat Bhirangi

PRINTED IN INDIA
by Rave India
A 27, Naraina Industrial Area, Phase II
New Delhi 110028

# Author's note

Any time is Salad Time! A bowl of fruit salad can give you a fresh start to a new day; mid-morning is the perfect time for a salad break; a salad at lunchtime is the antidote to those afternoon slumps; and what can be better than a colourful salad at the start of, or instead of, dinner!

Meals can begin with salads or end with them. A fresh salad in between courses cleanses the palate for what is to follow. There are light, crisp green salads, which are perfect for the petite appetite, and heavy-duty salads which will power you through a busy day. The versatile salad – rich in nutrients and packed with protein-rich ingredients, can be the perfect meal.

In this book, I have put together recipes for a range of irresistible salads to suit every mood and every occasion. There are everyday salads and ones that are dressed to impress; there are hot salads and cold salads, vegetarian and non-vegetarian salads and meal-in-a-bowl salads. Whatever the type of salad, I have kept in mind the 3 C's which describe the Perfect Salad – Colourful, Crisp and Chilled!

Here are some tips to make the perfect salad:

- Make sure all the ingredients are fresh and of the best quality.
- Use fruit, vegetables and greens which are unblemished, firm and in their prime.
- Use ingredients with a variety of colours which make the salad attractive. Chill all the ingredients well before using, and chill the salad once again after mixing.

- Wash greens before refrigerating. Remove the core (the hard part) and hold the greens upside down under running water. Drain on kitchen towels. Place in a plastic bag and refrigerate till ready to use.
- You can also let the greens soak in cold water for a while to let the mud and other impurities settle. Lift the greens out gently, dry and refrigerate.
- Use dark green leaves such as spinach and romaine lettuce, as they contain more vitamins. Cut salad ingredients, other than greens, into bite-size pieces.
- Do not cut greens with a knife - tear them into bite-size pieces with your fingers.
- Greens and vegetables will remain crispy and crunchy if you soak them in icy water for a while before making the salad.
- Do not overcook vegetables if using in a salad. They should retain a little crunch.
- Sprinkle apples, bananas, pears and avocados with lemon juice after peeling and cutting to prevent discolouration.
- Chill the serving bowl or salad plates so the salad will stay crisp for longer.
- For pasta salads, cook the pasta till *al dente* (cooked, but still firm to the bite). This will prevent the pasta from turning soggy when the dressing has been added.
- If using long noodles in a salad, rinse thoroughly after cooking to remove the excess starch and prevent noodles from sticking to each other.
- For a tastier potato salad, toss the boiled potatoes while still hot in vinaigrette (or a mixture of vinegar and oil), so that they absorb the dressing. Refrigerate when cold. Use baby potatoes in a potato salad for best results.
- Add tomatoes to a salad just before serving, or the salad will turn soggy.

- Add crunch and flavour to your salads with toasted seeds and nuts.

- Ingredients with strong flavours like pickled gherkins, olives, pickled onions, anchovies, Parmesan cheese, balsamic vinegar and sharp mustards add zing and bite to a bland salad.

- Turn a salad into a whole meal by adding cooked chicken, cold meats, prawns or paneer. Leftovers thrown into a salad add great flavour – wipe the gravy off paneer, chicken and meat, cut into small pieces and add to a salad.

- Yogurt makes a good substitute for sour cream in a dressing. Make sure you use less vinegar or lemon juice when using yogurt.

- For a low-fat mayonnaise dressing, replace part of the mayonnaise with fruit juice or pulp, or yogurt.

- Make a fruity dressing for green salads with fruit juices (orange, mango, apple) seasoned with salt, pepper and mustard.

- Dressings should moisten a salad, not smother it. Use just enough dressing to add flavour. You can always serve extra dressing on the side.

- To mix a dressing into a salad, toss the ingredients with two forks. Do not stir a dressing into a salad.

- Use a large bowl to mix salads – this will allow you to toss the ingredients freely and the dressing to coat the ingredients.

*Happy Cooking and Stay Cool !*

# Contents

# *Luncheon Salad*

300 grams boneless chicken cubes, boiled

2 red apples

4 celery stalks, trimmed

4 dark green cucumbers

100 grams processed cheese, cut into strips

3 tablespoons French Dressing (page 91)

1 cup Mayonnaise (page 92)

1 head of lettuce (optional)

5 red radishes (optional)

- Shred the chicken and set aside.
- Peel the apples and slice thinly. Soak in two cups of lightly salted water. Drain and set aside.
- Cut the celery into two-inch pieces. Slice thinly and soak in two cups of iced water. Drain and set aside.
- Soak the cucumbers in two cups of iced water. Wipe dry. Cut into two-inch pieces, then into strips.
- Place the apples, celery, cucumbers, shredded chicken and cheese in a bowl. Pour the French dressing over and toss to mix.

- Add the mayonnaise and mix well.
- Line a chilled salad bowl with the lettuce leaves. Spoon the salad into it and garnish with radish roses and serve immediately.

**Chef's Tip**
You can substitute apples with boiled potato cubes.

# Corn And Avocado Salad

10 baby corn cobs

1 large avocado

2 medium green capsicums, cut into strips

2 large tomatoes, seeded and cut into strips

2 medium cucumbers, cut into strips

**Dressing**

4 tablespoons honey

1 ½ tablespoons lemon juice

5-6 fresh mint leaves, roughly torn

5-6 black peppercorns, crushed

salt to taste

- Cut the baby corn into strips and blanch in boiling water. Drain.
- Gently peel and slice the avocado. Set aside a few slices for decoration.
- Mix the ingredients for the dressing in a large bowl.
- Add all the salad ingredients and toss well.
- Place in a refrigerator for twenty to thirty minutes to chill.
- Serve chilled, decorated with avocado slices.

## Chef's Tip
Drizzle lemon juice over the sliced avocado to prevent discolouration.

# Bread And Cheese Salad

4 thick slices day-old brown bread
225 grams processed cheese, cubed
¾ cup Garlic Dressing  (see below)
1 teaspoon chopped fresh thyme

8 one-inch pieces celery, sliced
   diagonally
4 large tomatoes, cut into wedges
celery leaves, to garnish

- Cut the bread into three-fourth-inch squares. Place in a large bowl.
- Mix the garlic dressing with the thyme and pour over the bread and toss to coat evenly.
- Add the celery and tomatoes and toss lightly. Add the cheese.
- Garnish with the celery leaves and serve at once.

### Garlic Dressing
Pour 6 tablespoons of olive oil into a bowl. Add 3½ tablespoons of lemon juice and 1 small crushed garlic clove. Whisk well adding a little salt and 3-4 freshly crushed black peppercorns.

# *Spinach Salad With Sour Cream*

2 bunches (450 grams) baby
   spinach leaves

2 medium tomatoes, sliced

4-5 asparagus spears, blanched and
   cut into 1-inch pieces

**Sour Cream Dressing**

1 cup thick cream

2 tablespoons olive oil

1 tablespoon lemon juice

salt to taste

7-8 black peppercorns, freshly
   crushed

1 teaspoon chopped onion

- Separate the spinach leaves. Wash in several changes of water, drain and spread out on a kitchen towel to dry. Cut into thin strips.

- Place the spinach, tomatoes and asparagus in a large bowl and place in a refrigerator for twenty minutes to chill.

- To make the sour cream dressing, whisk the cream till smooth. Add the olive oil, lemon juice, salt, peppercorns and onion.

- Pour the dressing over the spinach and vegetables and toss well to mix. Serve immediately.

13

# Russian Chicken Salad

2 (150 grams each) boneless chicken breasts, boiled and chopped

3 hard-boiled eggs

4 medium potatoes, boiled

1 medium onion, cut into ½-inch pieces

6 lettuce leaves, chilled

2 medium tomatoes, seeded and cut into ½-inch pieces

## Dressing

¾ cup Mayonnaise (page 92)

salt to taste

1 teaspoon white pepper powder

- Peel and cut the eggs lengthways into eight slices. Peel and cut the potatoes into half-inch cubes
- Combine the chicken, eggs, potatoes and onion in a large bowl.
- In a separate small bowl, combine the mayonnaise with salt and white pepper powder.
- Add the dressing to the chicken mixture and mix well.
- Line a bowl with lettuce leaves and spoon the salad into the bowl. Decorate with the chopped tomatoes, cover with cling film and place in a refrigerator for twenty-five to thirty minutes. Serve chilled.

# *Spicy Sausage Salad*

200 grams spicy chicken sausages, sliced

½ tablespoon olive oil

2 garlic cloves, sliced

1 medium onion, cut into rings

1 small red capsicum, cut into strips

6-8 lettuce leaves, roughly torn

salt to taste

6-8 black peppercorns, freshly crushed

3 stalks spring onion greens, sliced diagonally

* Heat the olive oil in a pan and sauté the garlic till brown.
* Toss the sausages, onion, capsicum, lettuce, salt and peppercorns together in a large bowl.
* Garnish with the spring onion greens and fried garlic. Serve immediately.

# Pina Colada Salad

2 thick fresh pineapple slices, diced

flesh of ½ tender coconut, sliced thinly

1 medium green capsicum, diced

½ cup boiled green peas

1 teaspoon red chilli flakes

**Dressing**

½ cup coconut milk

3 tablespoons grated fresh coconut

¼ cup thick cream

4 tablespoons pineapple juice

salt to taste

black pepper powder to taste

- Mix together the pineapple, coconut, capsicum and peas in a large salad bowl.
- Combine all the ingredients for the dressing in a small bowl.
- Just before serving, mix the dressing into the salad.
- Serve chilled, and sprinkle with red chilli flakes.

**Chef's Tip**
You can serve the salads in a hollowed-out pineapple shell for a more elegant effect.

# Coleslaw With Cottage Cheese

1 small cabbage, finely shredded

2 medium carrots, grated

100 grams cottage cheese (*paneer*), crumbled

½ cup drained yogurt

salt to taste

¼ teaspoon mustard powder

½ teaspoon white pepper powder

½ teaspoon sugar

¼ teaspoon caraway seeds (*shahi jeera*)

½ cup milk

1 tablespoon lemon juice

1 medium onion, grated

- Crumble the *paneer* and place in a blender with the drained yogurt, salt, mustard powder, white pepper powder, sugar and caraway seeds. Process till smooth. Add the milk and process again.
- Place the shredded cabbage in a bowl. Add salt to taste, the lemon juice and grated carrots and mix well.
- Squeeze out the water from the grated onion and add to the salad bowl.
- Add the *paneer* dressing and toss to mix. Serve at once.

# Chickpea And Red Capsicum Salad

3 cups boiled chickpeas, drained

2 red capsicums, roasted

12 black olives, stoned

1 tablespoon chopped fresh parsley

1 teaspoon grated orange rind

2 tablespoons orange juice

2-3 garlic cloves, crushed

salt to taste

4-6 black peppercorns, crushed

**Dressing**

2 tablespoons oil

- Mix all the ingredients for the dressing together.
- Toss the chickpeas while they are still warm into the dressing. Set aside to cool.
- Peel the capsicums. Halve them, remove the core and seeds and slice thinly.
- Stir in the capsicums, olives and half the parsley.
- Transfer the salad to a serving platter and garnish with the remaining parsley.

## Chef's Tip

To remove the skins of the capsicums easily, place the hot roasted capsicums in a plastic bag for a few minutes – the steam will loosen the skins.

# Piquant Potato Salad

750 grams baby potatoes
salt to taste

**Dressing**
3 tablespoons olive oil
1½ tablespoons white vinegar

7-8 peppercorns, crushed
1 teaspoon English mustard paste
2 pickled gherkins, finely chopped
1 tablespoon chopped fresh parsley

- Scrub the potatoes clean, wash and place in a large pan of boiling salted water. Boil for fifteen to twenty minutes, or till just tender. Drain.
- Meanwhile, make the dressing. Pour the olive oil and white vinegar into a small bowl; stir in salt to taste, crushed peppercorns, mustard paste, gherkins and parsley.
- Place the potatoes in a large bowl and pour the dressing over while the potatoes are still warm. Stir gently to coat thoroughly with the dressing.
- Leave to cool, but do not chill. Serve in a shallow dish at room temperature.

# Spicy Mexican Salad

1 cup sweet corn kernels, boiled

1 cup boiled red kidney beans (*rajma*), drained

1 small onion, cut into ½-inch pieces

1 small green capsicum, cut into ½-inch pieces

6 cooked chicken sausages, cut into ½-inch cubes

a handful of tortilla chips, crushed

**Dressing**

2 tablespoons chilli sauce

1 tablespoon tomato ketchup

1 tablespoon lemon juice

1 fresh red chilli, cut into thin slivers

a pinch of salt

- Place the corn, kidney beans, onion, capsicum and sausages in a large bowl. Toss lightly to mix.
- For the dressing, mix together the chilli sauce, tomato ketchup, lemon juice, red chilli and salt in a small bowl.
- Just before serving, spoon the dressing over the salad and toss well to mix.
- Serve, sprinkled with crushed tortilla chips.

# Lettuce, Garlic And Croutons in Vinaigrette

1 medium head of lettuce, chilled

4 slices white bread

2 tablespoons olive oil

3 garlic cloves, chopped

100 grams cottage cheese (*paneer*), cubed

6 cherry tomatoes, halved

**Dressing**

1 tablespoon vinegar

¼ cup olive oil

salt to taste

½ teaspoon mixed dried herbs

5-6 black peppercorns, freshly crushed

2 teaspoons chopped fresh parsley

- Preheat the oven to 180°C.
- Cut the bread into one-inch squares and toast in the oven till golden.
- Heat the olive oil in a non-stick pan; add the garlic and sauté till brown.
- Mix together all the ingredients for the dressing. Add the fried garlic.
- Place the roughly torn lettuce, croutons, *paneer* and cherry tomatoes in a large bowl. Pour the dressing over and toss to mix. Serve immediately.

# Chef's Salad

1 medium head of iceberg lettuce
3 hard-boiled eggs
4 black olives, stoned and chopped
4 green olives, stoned and chopped
4 red radishes, chopped

½ cup grated processed cheese
1 garlic clove, chopped
½ cup French Dressing (page 91)
2 medium tomatoes, quartered

- Tear the lettuce leaves roughly into bite-size pieces and soak in chilled water. Drain.
- Cut the eggs lengthways into eight slices.
- Place the lettuce in a bowl; add the olives, radishes, eggs, cheese and garlic.
- Pour the French dressing over the salad and toss well.
- Serve, garnished with tomatoes.

# Corn And Bean Twosome

1½ cups sweet corn kernels, boiled and drained

1½ cups boiled red kidney beans (*rajma*)

2 spring onions

salt to taste

black pepper powder to taste

**Dressing**

2 tablespoons Mayonnaise (page 92)

¾ tablespoon mustard paste

2 tablespoons tomato ketchup

½ teaspoon paprika

- Chop the spring onion bulbs and greens separately.
- Mix all the ingredients for the dressing with a small wire whisk. Place in a refrigerator to chill.
- Toss the corn, kidney beans and spring onion bulbs in a large bowl.
- Pour the dressing over and season with salt and pepper to taste.
- Sprinkle with the spring onion greens and serve immediately.

# Sprouted Matki And Moong Salad

¾ cup sprouted *matki*

¾ cup sprouted green gram (*moong*)

1 medium onion, chopped

1 medium green capsicum, chopped

1 medium tomato, seeded and
chopped

2 green chillies, chopped

2 teaspoons lemon juice

1½ teaspoons *chaat masala*

salt to taste

2 tablespoons chopped fresh
coriander leaves

- Mix the sprouted *matki* and *moong*, onion, capsicum, tomato and green chillies in a bowl. Cover with cling film and refrigerate for half an hour.
- For the dressing, mix together the lemon juice, *chaat masala* and salt.
- Add the dressing to the chilled salad just before serving.
- Garnish with coriander leaves and serve at once.

# *Tzatziki*

4 medium cucumbers

3 tablespoons chopped fresh mint
leaves + 1 sprig, to garnish

1 garlic clove, crushed

1 teaspoon caster sugar

1 cup drained yogurt, whisked

salt to taste

½ teaspoon paprika

- Peel the cucumber and cut in half lengthways. Remove the seeds and slice as thinly as possible.
- Combine the chopped mint, garlic, caster sugar and yogurt in a bowl.
- Mix the cucumbers with the yogurt. Add salt to taste.
- Serve chilled, garnished with a sprinkling of paprika and the sprig of mint.

# California Salad

1 large head of lettuce, roughly torn and soaked in chilled water

4 medium carrots, coarsely grated

18-20 cherry tomatoes, halved

4 celery stalks, thinly sliced

1 cup seedless raisins (*kishmish*)

1 cup almonds, blanched and halved

4 tablespoons *charoli* (*chironji*)

2 tablespoons roasted sesame seeds (*til*)

salt to taste

15-20 black peppercorns, freshly ground

**Dressing**

3 tablespoons extra-virgin olive oil

2 tablespoons cider vinegar

2 teaspoons honey

4 tablespoons orange juice

- Place all the salad vegetables, raisins, almonds, *charoli* and sesame seeds in a large bowl.
- Place all the dressing ingredients in a small glass jar and shake well to mix.
- Pour the dressing over the salad and toss well to mix.
- Serve chilled, sprinkled with salt and freshly ground peppercorns.

# Three Lettuce And Prawn Salad

1 head of iceberg lettuce
1 head of romaine lettuce
1 head of green leaf lettuce
8 jumbo prawns, peeled and deveined
salt to taste
7-8 black peppercorns, freshly crushed
2 tablespoons sesame seeds (*til*), toasted

**Dressing**
2 teaspoons lemon juice
1 tablespoon balsamic vinegar
2 tablespoons extra-virgin olive oil
1 teaspoon mustard paste
salt to taste

* Wash the lettuce leaves and drain well. Season the prawns with salt and crushed peppercorns and coat generously with the sesame seeds.

* Heat a non-stick frying pan. Gently cook the prawns, turning them from time to time, till golden on both sides.

* Mix together all the ingredients for the dressing in a small bowl.

* Tear the lettuce roughly and add to the prawns. Pour the dressing over, toss to mix and serve immediately.

# Apple And Cucumber Salad

1 medium apple

1 medium cucumber

1 tablespoon lemon juice

4 lettuce leaves

½ tablespoon salad oil

a generous pinch of red chilli flakes

4-5 fresh mint leaves

salt to taste

5-6 orange segments, halved

½ medium carrot, cut into thin strips

1 medium tomato, quartered and sliced

1 spring onion, sliced

- Core and cut the apple into quarters and cut again into thin slices with the skin on. Sprinkle half the lemon juice and mix lightly. Peel the cucumber and cut into one-inch long pieces.

- Trim the lettuce leaves, wash under running water and soak in chilled water, to keep them fresh and crisp.

- Mix the remaining lemon juice, salad oil, chilli flakes and mint leaves. Add salt to taste and whisk well.

- Drain the lettuce leaves and tear them into bite-size pieces. Make a bed of lettuce on a serving dish. Drizzle one-fourth of the dressing over the leaves.

- Combine the apple, cucumber, orange segments, carrot, tomato and spring onion in a bowl.

- Add the remaining dressing, toss to mix and spoon onto the bed of lettuce. Serve immediately.

# *Beetroot Salad With Yogurt*

1 large beetroot, blanched, peeled and thinly sliced

¾ cup yogurt

3 tablespoons Mayonnaise (page 92)

salt to taste

2½ teaspoons sugar

1 large apple, sliced

1 small head of lettuce, shredded

5 almonds, toasted and slivered

- Whisk the yogurt with the mayonnaise, salt and sugar.
- Combine the beetroot, apple and half the lettuce.
- Add the yogurt dressing and mix gently.
- Transfer to a serving bowl and serve, garnished with remaining lettuce and toasted almond slivers.

# Carrot And Apple Salad

3 medium carrots, coarsely grated

2 medium apples, cored and sliced

¾ tablespoon lemon juice

¾ tablespoon *charoli* (*chironji*)

2 tablespoons seedless raisins (*kishmish*)

6-8 cashew nuts, fried

**Dressing**

3 tablespoons salad oil

2 tablespoons lemon juice

a pinch of sugar

salt to taste

5-6 black peppercorns, freshly ground

- Sprinkle the apple slices with the lemon juice to prevent discolouration.
- Place the grated carrots in a large bowl. Add the apple, *charoli*, raisins and fried cashew nuts.
- Place all the ingredients for the dressing in a small glass jar and shake well to mix.
- Pour the dressing over the salad and toss lightly.
- Serve immediately.

# Chicken Salad

2 (150 grams each) boneless chicken
  breasts

salt to taste

1 teaspoon lemon juice

black pepper powder to taste

a pinch of MSG (optional)

1 celery stalk, sliced thinly

1 small apple

1 hard-boiled egg

2 medium carrots, thinly sliced,
  blanched

1 medium onion, thinly sliced

1 cup Mayonnaise (page 92)

4 lettuce leaves

* Boil chicken breasts in salted water for fifteen minutes. Cool and shred.
  Sprinkle lemon juice, a pinch of salt, pepper powder and MSG.

* Soak the celery in chilled water for ten minutes. Drain and wipe dry.

* Peel and core the apple and slice thinly. Soak in chilled, salted water for
  ten minutes; drain.

* Chop the egg white and pass the yolk through a sieve.

* Blanch the carrots in boiling water; drain and refresh in cold water.

- Place the chicken, celery, apple, egg white, carrots and onion in a bowl.
- Pour the mayonnaise over the ingredients and toss well. Season with salt and pepper.
- Arrange the lettuce in a serving plate and place the salad on it.
- Garnish with the sieved egg yolk and serve immediately.

# *Crunchy Celery And Cucumber Medley*

3 celery stalks, trimmed and
  chopped

2 small cucumbers, chopped

¾ cup pomegranate kernels

¾ cup halved seedless grapes

a few lettuce leaves

**Dressing**

½ cup yogurt, whisked

¾ teaspoon honey

¾ teaspoon mustard paste

salt to taste

black pepper powder to taste

* Place the celery, cucumber, pomegranate and grapes in a large salad bowl. Place in a refrigerator to chill thoroughly for at least half an hour.
* Mix together all the ingredients for the dressing.
* Just before serving, pour the dressing over the salad and toss well to mix.
* Serve on a bed of lettuce.

# Salade Nicoise

1 head of iceberg lettuce
4 medium potatoes
15 French beans
4 medium tomatoes, quartered

4 hard-boiled eggs, quartered
½ cup French Dressing (page 91)
10 black olives, stoned

- Tear the lettuce into bite-size pieces and soak in chilled water.
- Boil, peel and dice the potatoes. Cut the French beans into two-inch pieces. and blanch in boiling water. Drain and cool.
- Place the potatoes, French beans, tomatoes and eggs in a large bowl. Toss once to mix.
- Pour the French dressing over and using two forks, carefully toss the vegetables until they are thoroughly coated with the dressing.
- Arrange the chilled lettuce leaves on a large, shallow serving platter.
- Spoon the salad onto the lettuce leaves and garnish with black olives.
- Serve immediately.

# *Chinpen Noodle Salad*

2 (150 grams each) boneless chicken breasts

100 grams egg noodles

salt to taste

3 tablespoons sesame oil

1 spring onion, finely chopped

1 medium pickled gherkin, sliced

1 tablespoon light soy sauce

1½ tablespoons malt vinegar

1 green chilli, seeded and chopped

5-6 black peppercorns, crushed

2 tablespoons tahina (sesame seed paste)

1 teaspoon mustard powder

- Heat three cups of water in a pan. Add the chicken breasts and bring to a boil. Lower heat and simmer for five to six minutes, or until the chicken is tender and just cooked.

- Remove from heat and allow chicken to stand in the stock for fifteen minutes longer. Remove the chicken from the stock, cool and chop finely.

- Reheat the chicken stock and bring to a boil. Add a little salt, one tablespoon of sesame oil and the noodles and cook for three to four minutes, or until almost cooked. Remove, drain and spread out on a platter to cool.

- Mix the chicken together with the noodles, spring onion and pickled gherkin in a large mixing bowl and chill in the refrigerator.

- Combine the soy sauce, vinegar, green chilli, crushed peppercorns, salt and the remaining sesame oil in a small bowl. Add the sesame paste and mustard powder and mix well.

- Just before serving, toss the chilled salad in the mustard-sesame paste dressing till well mixed.

- Alternatively, serve the salad in individual salad plates or bowls with the dressing on the side.

# Green Jewels In A Bowl

¼ medium head of broccoli, separated into florets

8-10 French beans, sliced diagonally

1 medium green capsicum, cut into strips

1 large cucumber, halved and sliced diagonally

¾ cup bean sprouts

6 lettuce leaves, roughly torn and chilled

1 stalk spring onion greens, sliced

1 tablespoon roasted sesame seeds (*til*)

**Dressing**

1 tablespoon lemon juice

1 tablespoon olive oil

1 tablespoon soy sauce

3 teaspoons powdered sugar

7-8 black peppercorns, crushed

salt to taste

- Blanch the broccoli florets and French beans in boiling water. Refresh in cold water.
- Mix together the ingredients for the dressing and set aside.
- Place the broccoli, French beans, capsicum, cucumber, bean sprouts and lettuce in a large bowl.
- Pour the dressing over the salad and toss well to mix.
- Serve, sprinkled with the spring onion greens and roasted sesame seeds.

# Mango Salad

1 large green unripe mango

1 large head of lettuce

1 fresh red chilli, seeded and chopped

2 shallots, chopped

2 tablespoons lemon juice

1 tablespoon light soy sauce

1 cup chopped fresh coriander leaves

salt to taste

- Peel the mango and cut into long strips. Soak in iced water for ten minutes. Drain.
- Line a large salad bowl with the lettuce leaves.
- Combine the red chilli, shallots, lemon juice and soy sauce in a large bowl.
- Mix the mango with the dressing and add the coriander leaves. Add salt to taste.
- Transfer the salad to the bowl lined with the lettuce leaves. Serve immediately.

# Green Banana Salad

2 green unripe bananas

salt to taste

1 medium cucumber, chopped

2 celery stalks, thinly sliced

1 medium carrot, coarsely grated

1 small bunch lettuce leaves

**Dressing**

3 tablespoons olive oil

1 tablespoon vinegar

salt to taste

$\frac{1}{4}$ teaspoon black pepper powder

1 garlic clove, crushed

2 teaspoons mustard paste

- Peel the bananas and cook in boiling salted water for ten minutes, or until just tender.
- Drain, cool and cut crosswise into half-inch thick slices.
- Place all the ingredients for the dressing in a small glass jar and shake well to mix.
- Mix together the banana, cucumber, celery and carrot in a large bowl.
- Add the dressing and toss well to mix.
- Serve on a bed of lettuce.

# Green Papaya Salad

2 cups shredded green unripe
  papaya
4 garlic cloves
salt to taste
1 fresh red chilli, roughly chopped
4 cherry tomatoes, quartered

2 tablespoons lemon juice
2 tablespoons brown sugar
1 tablespoon fish sauce
½ tablespoon tamarind pulp
½ cup roasted peanuts, crushed

- Place the shredded papaya in a large bowl and crush lightly with a pestle.
- Crush the garlic cloves and salt with a mortar and pestle. Add the red chilli and cherry tomatoes and continue to crush lightly.
- Add the crushed garlic mixture to the papaya with the lemon juice and mix well.
- Crush the brown sugar, fish sauce and tamarind pulp with the mortar and pestle. Add to the papaya mixture and mix.
- Add the crushed roasted peanuts and toss to mix.
- Serve immediately.

# California Pista Pasta Salad

¼ cup pistachios, coarsely chopped

1 cup short pasta, boiled

2 medium tomatoes, chopped

6-8 baby spinach leaves

2 tablespoons Parmesan cheese powder

**Dressing**

3 tablespoons olive oil

1 tablespoon balsamic vinegar

a pinch of dried oregano

salt to taste

¼ teaspoon black pepper powder

- Mix together all the ingredients for the dressing in a large bowl.
- Add the pasta to the dressing and toss to mix.
- Add the tomatoes, spinach leaves and pistachios and mix well.
- Sprinkle with the Parmesan cheese powder and serve.

## Chef's Tip

You may use any short pasta shapes such as macaroni, fusilli or penne.

# French Bean And Sesame Salad

250 grams French beans, cut into thin diagonal slivers

2 tablespoons roasted sesame seeds (*til*)

1 small dark green, unpeeled cucumber, cubed

1 celery stalk, chopped

a few lettuce leaves

**Dressing**

2 tablespoons salad oil

2 tablespoons vinegar

½ teaspoon mustard paste

½ teaspoon sugar

1 pickled gherkin, minced

salt to taste

black pepper powder to taste

- Put all the ingredients for the dressing into a small glass jar and shake well. Place in a refrigerator till required.
- Steam the French beans for five minutes and drain. Leave to cool.
- Mix together the beans, cucumber and celery in a bowl.
- Just before serving, pour the dressing over the salad.
- Sprinkle with the sesame seeds and serve on a bed of lettuce.

# *Chickpea And Tahina Salad*

2 cups boiled chickpeas (*kabuli chana*)

½ tablespoon tahina (sesame seed paste)

½ cup Mayonnaise (page 92)

1 tablespoon olive oil

2 teaspoons lemon juice

salt to taste

black pepper powder to taste

1 medium cucumber, seeded and diced

1 medium tomato, seeded and diced

1 medium carrot, coarsely grated

- Place the tahina and mayonnaise in a small bowl.
- Whisk in the olive oil and lemon juice with a wire whisk. Add the salt and pepper powder to taste.
- Place the chickpeas, cucumber, tomato and carrot in a large bowl.
- Pour the dressing over and toss to mix. Serve immediately with sliced wholewheat or pita bread.

# Insalata Nuova Cucina

1 large head of iceberg lettuce
4-5 fresh button mushrooms
1 small yellow capsicum
1 small red capsicum
1 medium tomato
10-12 French beans, blanched
8 stuffed green olives
fresh basil sprigs, to garnish

**Dressing**
2 tablespoons balsamic vinegar
3 tablespoons olive oil
salt to taste
5-6 black peppercorns, crushed

- Dice all the vegetables and the olives and mix together in a large bowl.
- For the dressing, mix together the balsamic vinegar, olive oil, salt and crushed peppercorns.
- Pour over the salad and toss thoroughly to mix.
- Garnish with fresh basil sprigs.

**Chef's Tip**
You can add a few cooked prawns or cubes of chicken if desired.

# Christmas Coleslaw

1 small purple cabbage, shredded

1 small green cabbage, shredded

3 tablespoons crushed walnut kernels

½ cup Mayonnaise (page 92)

1 tablespoon Quick French Dressing (page 93)

salt to taste

$\frac{1}{8}$ teaspoon white pepper powder

2-inch celery stalk, chopped

½ medium apple, cut into thin strips

- Place the cabbages and two tablespoons of crushed walnuts in a large bowl.

- In a separate bowl, mix together the mayonnaise with the French dressing, salt, white pepper powder and celery.

- Pour the dressing over the cabbage mixture. Add the apple and toss gently to mix.

- Serve, sprinkled with the remaining crushed walnuts.

# Red Onion, Tomato And Pasta Salad

1 large onion, sliced thinly

4 medium tomatoes, quartered and seeded

3 cups short pasta of different shapes, cooked *al dente*

1 yellow capsicum, roasted

2 small zucchinis, sliced

salt to taste

a few sprigs of fresh basil, to garnish

**Dressing**

4 tablespoons olive oil

1 ½ tablespoons red wine vinegar

1 teaspoon Dijon mustard

½ teaspoon caster sugar

salt to taste

12-15 black peppercorns, crushed

½ cup roughly torn fresh basil leaves

- Cool the capsicum, peel and slice into strips.
- Blanch the zucchini and refresh in cold water.
- Mix together all the ingredients for the dressing.
- Drain the pasta well and transfer to a large serving bowl. Add the dressing and toss well.

- Add the capsicum, zucchini, onion and tomatoes; toss well to mix.
- Cover the bowl and leave to stand at room temperature for about thirty minutes to allow the flavours to develop.
- Serve, garnished with sprigs of basil.

# Pasta And Corn Salad

1 cup boiled elbow macaroni

1 cup sweet corn kernels, boiled

7-8 broccoli florets, blanched

8-10 cherry tomatoes

½ medium yellow capsicum, cut into strips

½ medium red capsicum, cut into strips

2 tablespoons olive oil

4 teaspoons vinegar

salt to taste

crushed black peppercorns, as required

a pinch of dried basil

- Place the macaroni, corn, broccoli, cherry tomatoes and capsicums in a deep bowl.
- Mix together the olive oil, vinegar, salt and peppercorns in a separate bowl.
- Pour the dressing over the salad and toss well to mix. Sprinkle with the dried basil.
- Chill for twenty minutes in a refrigerator and serve.

# *Indian Salad With Mango Dressing*

3 tinned pineapple slices, drained
  and cut into 1-inch cubes

1 medium unpeeled apple, cut into
  1-inch cubes

1 banana, peeled and cut into
  1-inch cubes

1 large tomato, seeded and
  quartered

1 medium green capsicum, cut
  into 1-inch cubes

1 orange, separated into segments

**Mango Dressing**

½ cup fresh mango pulp

½ cup thick yogurt, whisked

* Place all the salad ingredients in a large bowl, cover with cling film and
  place in a refrigerator to chill thoroughly.

* Meanwhile, make the mango dressing: mix together both the ingredients
  till smooth. Chill thoroughly.

* Just before serving, pour the dressing over the salad, mix well and serve
  chilled.

# *Mushroom And Cheese Salad*

10-12 fresh button mushrooms, quartered

100 grams processed cheese, cut into small cubes

4 large lettuce leaves, roughly torn

2 garlic cloves, chopped

3 tablespoons Vinaigrette (page 94)

1 tablespoon chopped fresh coriander leaves

- Place the mushrooms, cheese, lettuce and garlic in a bowl.
- Pour the vinaigrette over and toss to mix. Place in a refrigerator for twenty minutes.
- Garnish with coriander leaves and serve.

# Fattoush

1 medium green capsicum, cut into 1-inch cubes

1 medium tomato, cut into 1-inch pieces

1 medium cucumber, cut into 1-inch pieces

1 medium onion, cut into 1-inch pieces

2 tablespoons olive oil

2-3 bread slices, cut into 1-inch cubes

1 small head of iceberg lettuce

5-6 black olives, stoned

5-6 green olives, stoned

1-2 sprigs fresh parsley

**Dressing**

3 tablespoons olive oil

1 tablespoon vinegar

1 tablespoon lemon juice

salt to taste

½ teaspoon black peppercorns, crushed

1 tablespoon fresh parsley, chopped

1 teaspoon dried mint

- Heat the olive oil in a pan; add the bread cubes and sauté over medium heat to make golden croutons.
- To make the dressing, pour the olive oil into a bowl; add the vinegar, lemon juice, salt, crushed peppercorns, parsley and dried mint and whisk well.
- Tear the iceberg lettuce roughly and place in a large bowl. Add all the vegetables, onion, and black and green olives. Tear the parsley roughly and add to the bowl; toss well to mix.
- Just before serving, pour the dressing over, add the croutons and toss again.
- Serve immediately.

# Mango And Pineapple Salad

2 ripe mangoes, peeled and cut into ½-inch cubes

¹/₃ small pineapple, peeled, cored and cut into ½-inch cubes

½ small head of lettuce, torn into bite-size pieces

rock salt (*sendha namak*) to taste

1½ teaspoons *chaat masala*

¼ teaspoon lemon juice

2-3 black peppercorns, crushed

- Place the mangoes, pineapple and lettuce in a large bowl.
- Add the rock salt, *chaat masala* and lemon juice and toss well to mix.
- Sprinkle the crushed peppercorns over the salad and serve immediately.

# *Warm Red Cabbage Salad*

1 medium red cabbage, finely
   shredded

1 tablespoon butter

salt to taste

½ cup bean sprouts

1 small green capsicum, cut into
   strips

1 medium apple, cut into thin strips

**Dressing**

½ tablespoon honey

1 teaspoon red chilli flakes

6-8 black peppercorns, crushed

½ tablespoon lemon juice

- Heat the butter in a pan; add the cabbage and salt and toss over high heat for one minute. Set aside.
- Place the bean sprouts, capsicum and apple in a separate bowl and toss to mix.
- Place all the ingredients for the dressing in a small bowl and whisk well.
- Pour the dressing over the sprout mixture and toss to mix. Transfer to a serving platter.
- Arrange the tossed red cabbage in a ring around the sprout mixture. Serve immediately.

# Scandinavian Cucumber And Dill Salad

4 medium cucumbers

4 sprigs fresh dill (*suva*), chopped

salt to taste

4 tablespoons Sour Cream (page 78)

6-8 black peppercorns, ground

2 stalks spring onion greens, chopped

- Slice the cucumbers as thinly as possible, preferably in a food processor or with a slicer.

- Place the slices in layers in a colander set over a plate to catch the juices. Sprinkle each layer evenly, but not too heavily, with salt.

- Leave the cucumber to drain for upto two hours, then lay out the slices on a clean kitchen towel and pat them dry.

- Just before serving, mix the cucumbers with the dill, sour cream and freshly ground peppercorns.

- Serve immediately, garnished with spring onion greens.

# *Chilled Melon Ball Salad*

¼ watermelon

1 medium muskmelon

**Dressing**

1½ teaspoons lemon juice

2 tablespoons orange juice

3-4 black peppercorns, crushed

1 tablespoon roughly torn fresh
mint leaves

salt to taste

black salt to taste

- Using a Parisienne scoop (melon baller), scoop out small balls from the watermelon and the muskmelon. Discard all seeds.
- Place melon balls in a refrigerator to chill thoroughly.
- Mix together all the ingredients for the dressing. Pour over the melon balls and toss gently once or twice to mix. Spoon into the melon shells and serve immediately.

## Chef's Tip
To make a decorative melon bowl, cut the muskmelon in half. Scoop out small balls leaving a thick shell. Give a decorative zigzag edge using a small sharp knife.

# Grilled Chicken And Mushroom Salad

2 (150 grams each) boneless chicken breasts

6 large fresh button mushrooms

salt to taste

½ teaspoon black pepper powder

½ teaspoon mustard paste

½ teaspoon garlic paste

2 tablespoons oil

1 medium yellow capsicum

1 medium red capsicum

6 black olives, stoned and sliced

½ head of iceberg lettuce, roughly torn

**Dressing**

1 tablespoon olive oil

1½ tablespoons lemon juice

7-8 black peppercorns, crushed

2 teaspoons powdered sugar

salt to taste

- Marinate the chicken breasts in salt, pepper powder, mustard paste and garlic paste for twenty minutes.
- Mix together all the ingredients for the dressing.
- Grill the chicken breasts for ten to twelve minutes. Cool, slice and set aside.

- Brush the mushrooms with oil and grill for two minutes. Cut into quarters and set aside.

- Brush the yellow and red capsicums with oil and grill for ten minutes, turning them once or twice to cook evenly. Cut in half, remove the seeds, slice and set aside.

- Place the chicken, mushrooms, capsicums, olives and lettuce in a large bowl.

- Pour the dressing over the salad and toss well to mix.

- Serve immediately.

# Fruit And Capsicum Kachumber

2 medium apples, cored and sliced thinly

2 medium oranges

12-15 seedless green grapes, halved

12-15 seedless black grapes, halved

1 medium green capsicum, cut into strips

2 tablespoons lemon juice

1 medium cucumber, sliced thinly

2 medium tomatoes, seeded and cut into strips

2 spring onions, sliced thinly

**Dressing**

1 tablespoon chopped fresh coriander leaves

8-10 fresh mint leaves, roughly torn

2 green chillies, chopped

1½ teaspoons *chaat masala*

salt to taste

- Sprinkle one tablespoon of lemon juice over the apple slices to prevent discolouration.

- Peel the oranges and separate the segments. Remove the seeds and cut each segment in half.

- For the dressing, mix together the coriander leaves, mint leaves, green chillies, *chaat masala*, salt and remaining lemon juice.
- Toss the fruit and vegetables in the dressing and serve chilled.

# *Classic Greek Salad*

1 head of iceberg lettuce, roughly torn

1 medium cucumber, halved lengthways and sliced

4 medium tomatoes, cut into wedges

8 spring onions, sliced

10 black olives, stoned

100 grams feta cheese, diced

3 tablespoons white vinegar

2 tablespoons extra-virgin olive oil

salt to taste

10-12 black peppercorns, freshly ground

- Place the lettuce, cucumber, tomatoes, spring onions, olives and cheese in a large bowl.
- Whisk the vinegar and olive oil together in a small bowl. Add the salt and freshly ground peppercorns.
- Pour the dressing over the salad and toss well to mix.
- Serve immediately with crusty bread.

# *Broad Bean Salad*

400 grams broad beans (double beans), soaked overnight

2 cloves

2 tablespoons mixed dried herbs

1 onion, quartered

1 medium carrot, chopped

salt to taste

1 tablespoon French mustard

½ cup oil

1 garlic clove, chopped

1½ tablespoons chopped mixed fresh herbs

salt to taste

black pepper powder to taste

**Dressing**

2 tablespoons wine vinegar

- Tie the cloves and mixed dried herbs in a small piece of muslin to make a *bouquet garni*.
- Bring six cups of water to a boil in a large pan. Add the drained beans, *bouquet garni*, onion, carrot and salt.

- Cook till the beans are tender. Drain and discard the onion, carrot and *bouquet garni*, but reserve the cooking liquid. Keep the beans warm.

- Mix together all the ingredients for the dressing.

- Pour the dressing over the warm beans and toss well. Add a little of the reserved cooking liquid if the salad seems a little dry and serve warm.

**Chef's Tip**
You can use *rajma* or black-eyed beans instead of broad beans.

# Carrot Salad With Raisins, Nuts And Sour Cream

4 large carrots

½ cup seedless raisins (*kishmish*)

½ cup peanuts, coarsely crushed

salt to taste

5-6 black peppercorns, freshly
crushed

2 teaspoons grated lemon rind

1 tablespoon lemon juice

1 cup Sour Cream (see below)

- Place the carrots on ice for one hour. Grate them coarsely into a bowl.

- Add the raisins and peanuts and mix lightly.

- Sprinkle salt, peppercorns, lemon rind and lemon juice over the ingredients. Toss once or twice to mix.

- Pour the sour cream over and serve immediately.

**Sour Cream**
Whisk 1 tablespoon of lemon juice into 1 cup of fresh cream.
Add salt to taste. Use immediately.

# Pasta And Vegetable Salad

1 cup farfalle (butterfly-shaped pasta)

1 small brinjal, thinly sliced

1 medium onion, sliced

1 large tomato, peeled and cut into wedges

1 small red capsicum, sliced

1 garlic clove, sliced

1½ tablespoons olive oil

salt to taste

¼ teaspoon black pepper powder

a few lettuce leaves

2 tablespoons crumbled feta cheese

3-4 fresh basil leaves, roughly torn

**Dressing**

1½ tablespoons olive oil

3 tablespoons orange juice

a pinch of paprika

3-4 black peppercorns, freshly crushed

salt to taste

- Preheat the oven to 220°C.

- Arrange the brinjal, onion, tomato, capsicum and garlic in a single layer in an ovenproof dish. Drizzle with olive oil and season with salt and pepper powder. Cook in the oven for thirty to forty minutes, or until the vegetables begin to turn brown. Remove from the oven and set aside to cool.

- Cook the farfalle in plenty of boiling salted water till *al dente* (cooked but still firm to the bite). Drain and place farfalle in a bowl.

- Mix together all the ingredients for the dressing in a small bowl.

- Pour the dressing over the farfalle while still hot. Toss well and set aside to cool.

- Line a serving platter with lettuce leaves.

- To serve, place the farfalle in the centre of the platter. Arrange the cold roasted vegetables in a pile over the farfalle.

- Sprinkle the crumbled Feta cheese and basil leaves over the salad. Serve immediately.

# *Warm Red Curry Chicken Salad With Salsa Verde*

2 (150 grams each) boneless chicken breasts

2 large tomatoes, seeded and chopped

1 cup chopped fresh parsley

1 tablespoon lemon juice

¼ cup + 1 tablespoon olive oil

5-6 black peppercorns, freshly crushed

1½ tablespoons Thai Red Curry Paste (page 93)

salt to taste

2 heads of lettuce, roughly torn

- Remove the skin and cut the chicken breasts into thick slices.

- For the *salsa verde*, mix together the tomatoes, parsley, lemon juice, one-fourth cup of olive oil and crushed peppercorns in a bowl.

- Heat one tablespoon of olive oil in a large frying pan.

- Add the chicken slices and fry until golden brown and cooked through.

- Add the red curry paste and stir-fry for two minutes longer.
- Arrange a bed of lettuce on a serving platter.
- Pile the chicken slices on the lettuce and spoon the *salsa verde* over.
- Serve immediately.

# Gado-Gado

2 medium potatoes, boiled and
  peeled
15-20 French beans
2 medium carrots
1 medium cucumber
1 cup bean sprouts

**Peanut Sauce**

1 cup roasted peanuts
1 tablespoon grated jaggery
1 tablespoon tamarind pulp
½ teaspoon red chilli powder
salt to taste

- Cut the potatoes into one-inch fingers. Cut the French beans into one-inch pieces and the carrots into one-inch fingers. Blanch the French beans and carrots in boiling salted water. Drain and refresh in cold water. Cut the cucumber into one-inch fingers.
- Grind the ingredients for the peanut sauce with one-fourth cup of water to a smooth paste.
- Place the salad ingredients in a large bowl and add the peanut sauce.
- Toss well and refrigerate for twenty to thirty minutes.
- Serve chilled.

# *Tropical Mayo Delight*

2 medium tomatoes, seeded and cut into large chunks

2 medium potatoes, boiled, peeled and cut into 1-inch cubes

1 large green capsicum, cut into large chunks

2 thick fresh pineapple slices, chopped

1 large unpeeled apple, cored and chopped

2 celery stalks, chopped

½ cup Thousand Island Dressing (page 94)

salt to taste

black pepper powder to taste

2 lettuce leaves

- Combine the tomatoes, potatoes, capsicum, pineapple, apple and celery in a large mixing bowl.
- Add the Thousand Island dressing and mix well. Add salt and pepper powder to taste. Place in a refrigerator to chill.
- Serve on a bed of lettuce.

# Macaroni And Sausage Salad

2 cups boiled and drained macaroni

4 chicken sausages, fried and chopped

1 pickled gherkin, minced

1½ tablespoons French Dressing (page 91)

½ cup cream

½ cup Mayonnaise (page 92)

salt to taste

a pinch of sugar

2 hard-boiled eggs, peeled and sliced

¼ teaspoon paprika

- Place the macaroni and pickled gherkin in a bowl and mix in the French dressing. Place in a refrigerator to chill.
- Meanwhile, whisk together the cream and mayonnaise in a small bowl. Add salt to taste and a pinch of sugar.
- Add the sausages to the macaroni and pour the dressing over.
- Transfer to a deep salad bowl and garnish with slices of boiled egg and a sprinkling of paprika. Serve immediately.

# *Pepper Slices With Cream Cheese*

1 red capsicum

1 yellow capsicum

1 green capsicum

¾ cup cream cheese

3 slices tinned pineapple, drained and crushed

¾ cup Mayonnaise (page 92)

salt to taste

10-12 black peppercorns, crushed

20 almonds, chopped

4 lettuce leaves

- Cut a piece from the stem end of the capsicums. Remove the seeds and the membranes.
- Beat the cream cheese till smooth; add the pineapple, mayonnaise, salt, crushed peppercorns and almonds.
- Stuff the capsicums with the cheese mixture, cover and chill for at least twelve hours.
- Slice each capsicum with a hot, sharp knife and place them on ice.
- Serve in a platter on a bed of lettuce leaves.

# Rice Salad

1 cup steamed rice

3 tablespoons Quick French Dressing (page 93)

6 red radishes, cut into thin round slices

1 medium capsicum, cut into thin strips

1-inch piece leek, shredded

1 small cucumber, thinly sliced

1 small carrot, cut into thin strips

2 pickled gherkins, shredded

salt to taste

1 tablespoon lemon juice

1 teaspoon red chilli flakes

1 tablespoon chopped fresh parsley

- Mix the French dressing into the steamed rice while still warm. Leave to cool.
- Mix in the radishes, capsicum, leek, cucumber, carrot and pickled gherkins.
- Add the salt, lemon juice and red chilli flakes and mix well.
- Transfer to a flat dish and garnish with parsley. Serve immediately.

# French Dressing

6 tablespoons olive oil

¼ teaspoon paprika

¼ teaspoon salt

¼ teaspoon mustard powder

1 teaspoon sugar

2 tablespoon vinegar or lemon juice

1 garlic clove

- Combine one tablespoon of olive oil, the paprika, salt, mustard powder, sugar and one tablespoon of vinegar or lemon juice in a bowl.
- Beat well with a wire whisk until smooth. Add two more tablespoons of olive oil and beat well again.
- Add one more tablespoon of vinegar or lemon juice, three more tablespoons of olive oil and the garlic. Mix well.
- Place the dressing in a jar and store in a cool place. You may remove the garlic after six or seven days.
- Shake the dressing well before using. Makes about ½ cup.

# *Mayonnaise*

| | |
|---|---|
| 1 egg yolk | ¼ teaspoon sugar |
| salt to taste | 1 teaspoon vinegar |
| ¼ teaspoon white pepper powder | 1 cup oil |
| ¼ teaspoon French mustard | 1 teaspoon lemon juice |

- Place the egg yolk, salt, white pepper powder, mustard, sugar and vinegar in a clean bowl and mix thoroughly with a whisk. Alternatively, process the mixture in a blender.

- Add the oil, a little at a time, whisking or blending continuously, until all the oil is incorporated.

- Add the lemon juice and adjust seasoning.

- Store in an airtight jar in the refrigerator.

# Quick French Dressing

½ cup olive oil

1½ tablespoons vinegar

1 teaspoon mustard powder,

½ teaspoon freshly crushed black peppercorns

salt to taste

+ Combine all the ingredients in a glass jar. Close tightly with the lid and shake well to mix.

# Thai Red Curry Paste

8 dried red chillies

4-inch lemon grass stalk

4 teaspoons coriander seeds

2 teaspoons cumin seeds

6 black peppercorns

2 medium onions, chopped

4 garlic cloves, chopped

salt to taste

+ Grind together the red chillies, lemon grass, coriander seeds, cumin seeds, peppercorns, onions, garlic and salt with a little water to a fine paste.

+ Store in the refrigerator where it will keep for a week to ten days.

# Thousand Island Dressing

¾ cup Mayonnaise (page 92)

1 tablespoon tomato ketchup

1 teaspoon Tabasco sauce

3-4 green olives, stoned and chopped

2-3 pickled onions, chopped

2 pickled gherkins, chopped

- Mix together the mayonnaise, tomato ketchup and Tabasco sauce in a bowl.
- Add the olives, pickled onions and gherkins and mix well.

# Vinaigrette

½ cup olive oil

2 tablespoons vinegar

1 teaspoon mustard paste

6-8 black peppercorns, crushed

salt to taste

- Combine all the ingredients in a glass jar. Close tightly with the lid and shake well to mix.

# Index

**Vegetarian Recipes**